SWIM AWAY! SWIM AWAY! THE GREAT WHITE SHARK IS AFTER ME!

ANIMAL BOOK 4-6

Children's Animal Books

Speedy Publishing LLC

40 E. Main St. #1156

Newark, DE 19711

www.speedypublishing.com

Copyright 2017

In this book, we're going to cover fascinating facts about the Great White Shark. So, let's get right to it!

Even though the great white shark isn't the largest shark in our oceans, it's probably the most dangerous predatory shark. The word "predatory" means that it is a very aggressive hunter and has an enormous appetite.

THE GREAT WHITE SHARK

The great white shark is a huge powerful fish. Most fish are cold-blooded, but great white sharks are warm-blooded. They can adapt to different water temperatures. This is one of the reasons that they are such fast swimmers.

WHAT DO THEY EAT?

Great white sharks are carnivores, which simply means they are meat-eaters. They have powerful sharp teeth but they don't chew. They just tear off big hunks and swallow them in one piece. Even though they are fish themselves, younger sharks have a diet that consists of large fish, which are smaller than they are, like tuna.

Favorite foods for adult great white sharks are sea lions as well as seals. They attack them in the water and have been known to jump up on ice or land to get them as well. They eat seabirds, dolphins, and have been known to attack and eat whales.

HOW DO THEY HUNT?

Scientists have been studying how great white sharks hunt for decades. One place they can be observed in action is at the Farallon Islands. Here, off the coast of San Francisco, the sharks come in close to shore to hunt seals. They alter their hunting, based on the species they're attacking.

When going after elephant seals, great whites will attack them from below and behind. Elephant seals are huge creatures that swim well when underwater. However, at the water's surface they are less than graceful. Their awkwardness here gives the great whites an opportunity to attack. They bite the animal until it bleeds to death. Then, they come back to feast on it.

California sea lions are smaller than elephant seals, but they are still excellent swimmers and graceful underwater. Great whites go after their

underbellies and then pull the seals down under the surface until they stop thrashing. Baby seals are grabbed either at the water's surface or on land and sometimes eaten whole.

IS IT A MANEATER?

Great white sharks have a bad reputation as maneaters. Although it's true that great whites have attacked more swimmers than any other type of shark, they don't hunt people. More than likely, they mistake the swimming person as a seal or another choice food.

A shark might take a bite before it decides that it doesn't like the taste. By that time, the swimmer is seriously injured or killed since the bite is 20-30 pounds of their flesh.

Despite the image of great white sharks in movies or television, great white shark attacks on people are very rare. We have too many bones and sharks prefer blubbery types of meat. Unlike many other types of creatures, sharks are not too territorial.

Even if you're swimming close to them, generally they'll not pursue you. Some people get very agitated when they see sharks in the water. The thrashing around gets the shark's attention because they think you're an injured animal. If you're calm and just slowly swim away, more than likely they won't swim toward you.

ARE GREAT WHITE SHARKS ENDANGERED?

In 1975, a famous blockbuster movie called Jaws hit theaters. It was about a great white that went after people as food. The movie wasn't a true picture of great whites, but fisherman started to go after the sharks to kill them and hunters went after its teeth and jaws as hunting trophies.

By the early 90s, the great white populations had become vulnerable, which simply means they were at risk to go extinct. Some countries took action to protect this amazing species. South Africa, followed by Namibia, created laws to ensure the shark wouldn't die out. Australia and the United States did the same.

As of 2014, marine biologists have reported that the numbers of great whites are increasing. It's believed that there are about 5,000 that swim along the East coast of the United States as well as another large population of 2,400 or more along California's coastline.

This doesn't mean that the great white is out of danger. It is still targeted by trophy hunters for its fins, teeth, and jaws. Every time a person is bitten, attacked, or killed, the media attention increases and people go after the great whites to kill them.

The truth is that great whites are apex predators, which simply means they are at the top of the food chain. Their presence is vital to keeping populations of other ocean creatures in balance. Our oceans wouldn't have the biodiversity they have without the presence of sharks.

DO GREAT WHITE SHARKS HAVE ANY PREDATORS?

The greatest nonhuman threat to great white sharks is other great white sharks. Yes, it's true that sometime a super-sized shark will go after a smaller-sized shark for lunch. Once they decide to attack, they swim powerfully by moving their tails rapidly from side to side. Their torpedo-like shape helps them to gain quick speed in the water and they can swim in spurts up to 40 miles per hour.

People that overfish them for their fins and teeth are a tremendous threat as well. About 70 great white attacks are reported worldwide every year, but people kill millions of sharks of all types yearly. It's clear that we're more a threat to great white sharks than they are to us.

HOW LARGE DO THESE FISH GET?

Great white sharks are massive ocean creatures. They can get up to 23 feet or 7 meters long and can weigh up to 5,000 pounds or 2,268 kilograms. When they are born they are already 4 or 5 feet long. The colors on their bodies help them to stay camouflaged in the water.

They are usually dark blue, brown or shades of dark grey bordering on black. They blend in with the ocean floor and their white bellies and sides blend in with sunlight and water when viewed from underneath them.

WHAT BIG TEETH YOU HAVE

These huge fish are known for their enormous teeth. They have many rows of teeth and it's not unusual for them to have as many as 300 very jagged teeth at one time. Over the course of their lives, they may lose and replace as many as 1,000 teeth. Their teeth are only used for biting and tearing, not for chewing.

Their teeth when upright are three inches tall. Their scientific name is Carcharodon Carcharias, which translates to "sharp teeth." In order to taste their food they use a tongue made of cartilage that's called a basihyal.

HOW DO THEY BREATHE?

Just like most other types of fish, great white sharks breathe through their gills. They have to have water continuously passing over their gill slits. This means if they don't keep swimming, they'll drown.

WHERE DO THEY LIVE?

Great whites have been found breaching on the surface of the water, which simply means they jump high out of the water. They've also been found as deep as 800 feet below the surface.

They travel along the coastlines of Australia and South Africa. They can also be found along the northeastern and California coasts of the United States. They like warm and salty seas.

ARE THEY SOCIAL?

Great white sharks do travel in groups called schools or shoals. If one shark has a tuna and another wants it, they will slap each other to get what they want. They don't as a rule bite each other, since one bite will disable their fellow shark.

HOW DO THEY GIVE BIRTH?

Unlike many other types of fish, female sharks carry their fertilized eggs internally. They'll give birth to one to twelve pups that are fully formed and ready to swim and take care of themselves. They have to swim away quickly because if they don't, their mothers will sometimes eat them. Great whites can live in the wild for up to 70 years.

WHY ARE THEY SUCH GOOD HUNTERS?

One of the things that's very scary about great white sharks is that they sense one drop of blood in 25 gallons or 95 liters of water. They can detect a small amount of blood from up to 3 miles or 4.8 kilometers away.

Sharks have excellent senses of hearing and smell. They also have good eyesight. They also have an additional sensing organ that is called the *Ampullae of Lorenzini*. This organ helps them to sense electrical

impulses of ocean creatures as well as boats or other mechanisms that give off electrical vibrations. Even if a creature is completely hidden on the bottom of the ocean, a great white can tell that it's there.

wesome! Now you know more about the Great White Shark, the most dangerous predatory shark. You can find more Animal books from Baby Professor by searching the website of your favorite book retailer.

Visit

BABY PROFESSOR
EDUCATION KIDS

www.BabyProfessorBooks.com
to download Free Baby Professor eBooks
and view our catalog of new and exciting
Children's Books